MUY CALIENTE!

Afro-Cuban Play-Along CD & Book

FEATURING:

Rebeca Mauleón - Keyboards and Coro
Oscar Stagnaro - Bass
Orestes Vilató - Timbales, Percussion and Coro
Edgardo Cambon - Congas, Percussion and Coro
Carlos Caro - Bongos, Percussion and Coro

OVER 70 MINUTES OF SMOKIN' LATIN GROOVES!

Stereo separation so bass or piano can be eliminated.
Practice with the masters!

Publisher & Editor - Chuck Sher
Musical Editor & Transcriber - Rebeca Mauleón
Music Copyist - Chuck Gee
Cover Design - Attila A. Nagy, Cotati, CA
Cover photos - David Garten
Recorded and Mixed at O Studio, El Cerrito, CA
Mastered at Paul Stubblebein Mastering, San Francisco, CA

About The Musicians

That **Rebeca Mauleón** is one of the world's greatest Latin pianists will be evident to anyone who listens to t[CD. Her encyclopedic knowledge of the various styles comprising "Latin music" and her pure joy in perpetuating t[music is evident here on every track. She is also the world's foremost Latin music educator—having written two of t[essential books documenting the history and structure of Afro-Cuban music, "The Salsa Guidebook For Piano A[Ensemble" and "101 Montunos", both published by Sher Music Co. She has recorded and performed with everyo[from Carlos Santana to Tito Puente, from Mickey Hart's Planet Drum to her own ensemble, "Round Trip".

Oscar Stagnaro also has the honor of being both a world-class player and teacher of Latin music. He is [Associate Professor Of Bass at Berklee College Of Music in Boston and the co-author of the forthcoming volun["The Latin Bass Book"—the definitive work on the subject, to be published in the year 2000 by Sher Music Co. [mastery of both traditional and modern bass styles has made him one of the elite of Latin bassists. He is currently t[bassist with Paquito D'Rivera and has recorded with such ensembles as The United Nations Orchestra and The Cari[bean Jazz Project. His first CD under his own name, "Mariella's Dream" was recently released on the Songasaur[label.

Orestes Vilató is one of the originators of modern timbales playing and is still a master in his prime, as you c[tell from this CD. He has recorded with virtually the entire pantheon of Salsa stars (over 300 albums) from Ed[Palmieri, Cheo Feliciano and Ray Barretto to Rubén Blades, Celia Cruz and Cal Tjader. He was a founding member [the Fania All-Stars, the Tipica '73 Orchestra and Los Kimbos and was nominated for a Grammy Award in 1995 for [performance on the CD "Ritmo Y Candela", along with Changuito and Patato. They don't come any better th[Orestes.

Edgardo Cambon is one of the most in-demand percussionists and singers in the San Francisco Bay Area, a[this CD shows you why. His recording credits include dates with Jesus "Chucho" Valdéz, Carlos Santana, Clau[Gomez, Keith Terry and "Crosspulse", Michael Spiro, Sovoso, Jackie Rago and Campana, Sol y Luna, Omar Sosa a[his own salsa band, "Candela".

Carlos Caro is the youngest member of the rhythm section and the most recent arrival, having immigrated [the United States from Cuba in 1995. In Cuba he played with Opus 13, Paulito y su Elite, and Grupo Clave, as well [the Mexico City Philharmonic enroute to settling in California. He now plays with several Bay Area bands, includi[QBA, Avance and Ritmo y Armonia.

Edgardo Cambon, Orestes Vilató, Rebeca Mauleón, Carlos Caro, Oscar Stagnar[

Sobre Los Músicos

Que **Rebeca Mauleón** es una de las grandes pianistas latinas en el mundo es evidente para cualquiera que escuche este CD. Su conocimiento eciclopédico de los varios estilos que comprenden la música latina y su puro disfrute en perpetuar esta música son obvios en cada tema. Mauleón es también la más sobresaliente educadora de esta música en el mundo, contando en su curriculum haber escrito dos de los libros esenciales que documentan la historia y extructura de la música afrocubana: "The Salsa Guide Book for Piano and Ensemble" y " 101 Montunos," ambos publicados por Sher Music Co. Mauleón ha grabado y actuado con diversos artistas desde Carlos Santana hasta Tito Puente, incluyendo el proyecto Planet Drum con Mickey Hart y su propio Ensemble, "Round Trip."

Oscar Stagnaro tiene el honor de ser un músico y profesor de clase mundial en el género de la música latina. Es profesor asociado de bajo en el Colegio de Música de Berklee en Boston, y co-autor del próximo volumen "The Latin Bass Book," el cual es un trabajo definitivo que será publicado en el año 2000 por Sher Music Co. Su maestría en los dos estilos "tradicional" y "moderno" del bajo lo ponen en la élite de los bajistas latinos. Actualmente es el bajista del grupo de Paquito D'Rivera, y ha grabado con la Orquesta de las Naciones Unidas y The Caribean Jazz Project. Su primer CD bajo su propio nombre, "Mariella's Dream" fué recientemente lanzado al mercado por el sello Songasaurus.

Orestes Vilató es uno de los creadores de la manera moderna de tocar el timbal, y continua siendo un maestro en la mejor etapa de su carrera como pueden comprobar en este CD. Ha grabado virtualmente con el panteón entero de las estrellas de la Salsa (más de 300 albums), desde Eddie Palmieri, Cheo Feliciano y Ray Barretto hasta Rubén Blades, Celia Cruz y Cal Tjader. Vilató fue miembro fundador de la Fania All Stars, La Orquesta Típica 73 y los Kimbos, y fue nominado al premio Grammy en 1995 por su presentación en el CD "Ritmo y Candela" junto a Changuito y Patato. No hay nada mejor que Orestes Vilató.

Edgardo Cambón es uno de los cantantes y percusionistas más solicitados en San Francisco y el Area de la Bahía, y este CD muestra por qué. Sus créditos de grabaciones incluyen trabajos con Jesús "Chucho" Valdéz, Carlos Santana, Claudia Gómez, Keith Terry and Crosspulse, Michael Spiro, Sovoso, Jackie Rago and Campana, Sol y Luna, Omar Sosa, y su propio grupo "Candela."

Carlos Caro es el miembro más joven de la sección rítmica, habiendo imigrado a los Estados Unidos de America desde Cuba en 1995. En Cuba tocó con la Orquesta Opus 13, Paulito y su Elite y grupo Clave, así como la Orquesta Filarmonica de México antes de establecerse en California. Actualmente toca con varias orquestas de música latina en el Area de la Bahía, entre ellas QBA, Avance, y Ritmo y Armonía.

Musical Editor's Foreword

When musicians get together and find the groove, it is obvious to everyone who comes within hearing range. As players on this recording, our intention was to demonstrate the delicate balance which exists in Afro-Caribbean music between stability and variation, so that any instrumentalist (or even vocalist) could not only play along with us, but feel free to improvise. As with any style of music, a solid groove is essential, and in Latin music in particular, you must remember that this music is primarily for dancing. Of course, it was also our hope to convey the excitement and joy we feel in playing this music, and to share these feelings with you. As you listen, imagine the possibilities we leave open: add a melody, a *coro* or a *moña* (see below), or get up and dance!

The tunes in this recording represent a few of the numerous popular styles that any Latin player should have under his/her belt. It is well worth the time and energy to go further and explore this music, its history and its never-ending evolution. In the meantime, here are some basic terms and tools which will help you in using this book/CD. (For more information, please consult the "Salsa Guidebook for Piano and Ensemble," published by Sher Music Co.)

About the Charts ~

All of the tracks include their rhythmic style, *clave* direction and key. Any tune which alternates styles will indicate these changes within the chart, or may list an alternate style in parentheses at the top. Any tune listed as a "charanga" infers that it is a style which would typically be played by a *charanga* orchestra, and also defines how the percussion parts are played. Notice that these tunes do not have bongos or bongo bell; rather, the main rhythmic structure is played by congas (sometimes only one drum), timbales (playing quarter-notes or eighth-notes on the cha-cha bell), and most importantly, the güiro.

Mini Glossary of Terms ~

Abanico - The rim shot and roll of the timbales.

Bomba - An Afro-Puerto Rican musical and dance style, as well as the drum often used to play it.

Bota - A term established by Cuban percussionist Changuito to refer to a particular breakdown section within the *songo* genre.

Cáscara - 1. The shell of the timbales; 2. The pattern played on the timbales, as well as other instruments, which is derived from Cuban rumba.

Cha-cha-chá - A musical and dance style developed from the Cuban danzón by violinist Enrique Jorrín in the early 1950s. It was initially interpreted by *charanga* orchestras.

Charanga - A style of instrumentation developed in Cuba of European origin, consisting of strings, flute, and a rhythm section containing piano, bass, timbales, conga(s) and güiro.

Chékere - A beaded gourd of West African origin traditionally used in the interpretation of sacred music.

Clave - 1. A Cuban instrument (called the "claves") made of polished, rounded wooden sticks, struck together; 2. The rhythmic patterns played by the *clave* instrument, as well as any other instrument. In Cuban music, there are several common *clave* patterns, including *son clave*, *rumba clave* and 6/8 *clave*.

Coro - The chorus, as well as the refrain of a song.

Guaguancó - One of the styles of Cuban *rumba*.

Guaracha - A musical style developed during the 1930s in Cuba, characterized by increased complexity in the bass structure of the *son* and its derivations. The *guaracha* is perhaps the most common rhythmic style associated with the genre known as "salsa."

Güira - The metal scraper instrument commonly used in Dominican merengue.

Güiro - The gourd scraper instrument used in most styles of Cuban and other Latin music.

Mambo - 1. The section added to the Cuban *danzón* form during the 1940s; 2. An up-tempo style popularized with the Cuban big band format, which blended elements of North American jazz with Cuban rhythm; 3. The section within an arrangement which features new, often multi-layered material (much like a bridge).

Merengue - A musical and dance style from the Dominican Republic, traditionally played on *tambora*, *güira* and accordion.

Moña - A term used to refer to horn lines within a *mambo* section of a tune, somewhat like a "shout" in American jazz

Track #1
Tuning Notes

NOTE: If the bass is too loud on your system, use the Balance control on your stereo to get the proper balance. Thanks!

Track #2

Guaracha 2-3

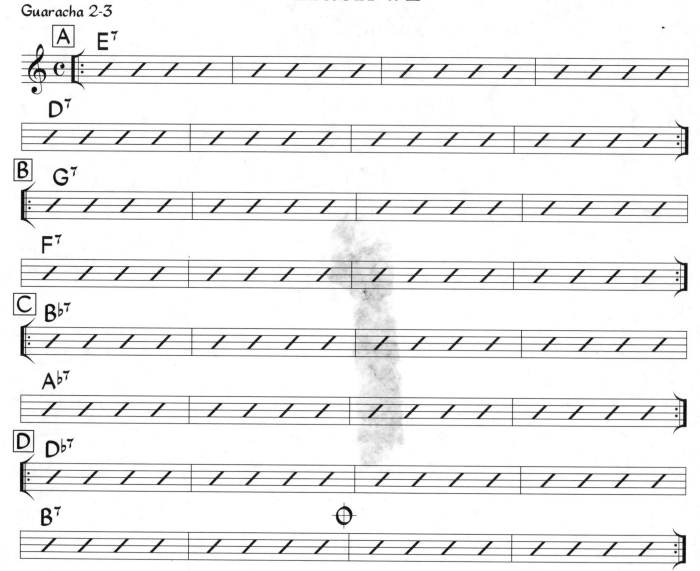

Play ⒶⒷⒸⒹ *(w/ repeats),*
then, D.C. al Coda (w/ repeats)

Sample piano and bass at letter A

Track #3

Bomba / Guaracha 3-2

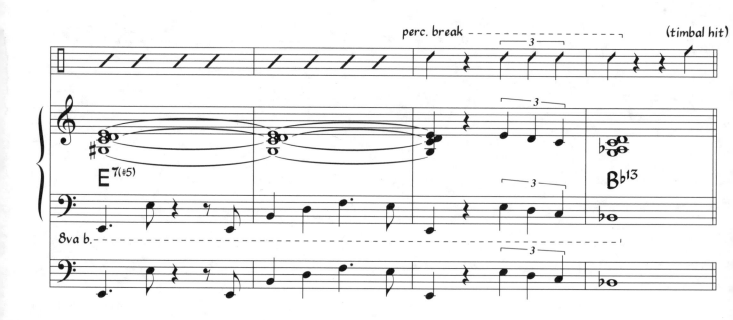

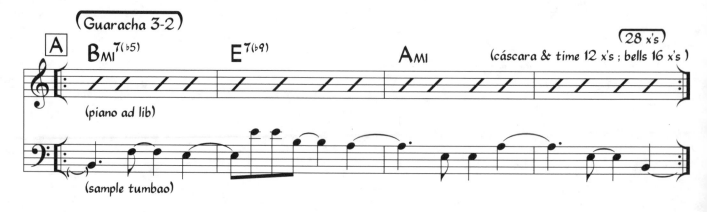

B (Bomba)

(Vamp and fade)

Track #4

Track #5

Cha-cha-chá

Cha cha chá   pa - ra que bai - len,   cha cha chá   pa - ra que go - cen.

Track #6

Track #7

Guaracha 2-3

Track #8

Track #9

Track #10

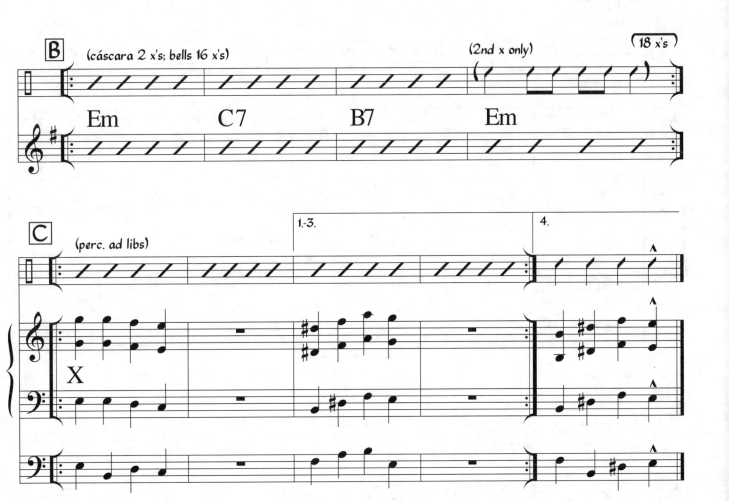

Track #11

Sample bass, 1st x at letter A

Sample piano at letter A toward end of section)

Track #12

Track #13

Track #14

C Breakdown section - "bota" bell ad lib

(rumba clave)

Am⁹   Am⁹ D⁹   Gma⁷   Bm⁹ E⁷(♭9)(♯5)

(hit and slide on all strings)

Am⁹   Am⁹ D⁷(♯9)(♯5)   Gma⁷   Bm⁹   E⁷(♯5)

(Vamp and fade)

D Am⁹/D   Am⁹ D⁷(♭9)(♯5)   Gma⁷/D   Bm⁹   E⁷(♭9)(♯5)/D

(sample tumbao)

Track #15

34

Sample piano and bass, 1st x at letter A

Sample piano and bass at letter B on repeat

Track #16

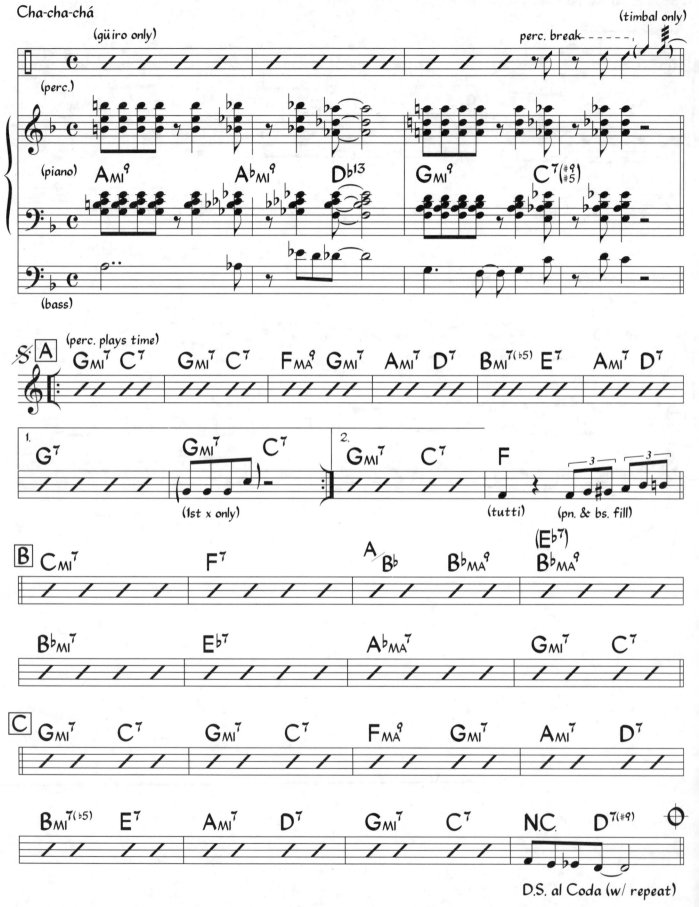

D.S. al Coda (w/ repeat)

Track #17

Sample piano and bass, 3rd x at letter A

Sample piano and bass, 7th x at letter C

Track #18

Track #19

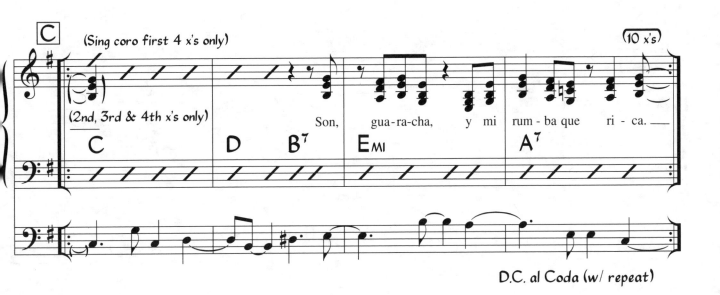

D.C. al Coda (w/ repeat)

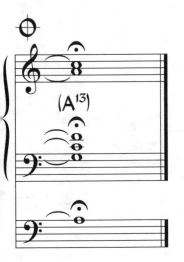

Track #20

Sample bass, 1st x at letter [A]

Track #21

Fast Guaracha 3-2
(Guaguancó Intro)

$A\flat^{13}_{SUS}$ $A\flat^{13}$ $D\flat^{6}_{9}/A\flat$ $F^{7(alt.)}$

(guaracha feel 3-2)

C $B\flat_{MI}(MA7)$ $A\flat_{MI}(MA7)$

$B\flat_{MI}(MA7)$ $A\flat_{MI}^{7}$ $D\flat^{7}$

$A\flat_{MI}^{7}$ $D\flat^{7}$ $G\flat_{MA}^{7}$ B^{6}_{9}

$C_{MI}^{7(\flat5)}$ $F^{7(alt.)}$ ⊕ $B\flat_{MI}(MA7)$

D.S. al Coda (w/ repeat)

⊕ $B\flat_{MI}$ $A\flat_{MI}^{7}$ $D\flat^{7}$ **D** $G\flat$ F^{7}

$B\flat_{MI}$ $A\flat_{MI}^{7}$ $D\flat^{7}$

(Vamp and fade)

Track #22

48

Sample piano and bass, 13th x at letter A

Sample piano and bass, 29th x at letter A

Track #23

Timba-Funk 3-2

(güira only)

(perc.)

(bass) (thumb/slaps)

(timbales fill)

(time 3-2; congas enter 3rd x)

A | DMI11 | C13SUS | | Bb9 | A7(b9#5) | DMI11 | 4 x's |

(pn. play chords) (bass continues similar figures)

(pn. plays montuno)

B | DMI | (G7) | C | Bb | A7 | DMI |

(vocals 8va b.)

Pa - ra to - car el ba - jo, hay que po - ner - le sa - bor. Si

DMI (G7) C Bb A7 DMI

___ quie-res to-car el ba - jo, el rit - mo lo pon-go yo.

C | DMI | G7 | C | Bb A7 | 1.-3. DMI | 4. DMI |

(pn. & bs. play similar figures)

D | DMI | G7 | C | Bb | A7 | DMI | Lo

que trai - go_es pa - ra go-zar a - sí que_hé - cha - te pa - cá.

DMI G7 C | 1.-3. Bb A7 DMI | 4. Bb A7 | DMI

Lo a - sí que_hé-cha-te pa - cá.

Latin Music Books & CDs from Sher Music Co

The Latin Real Book (C, Bb or Eb)

The only professional-level Latin fake book ever published! Over 570 pages. Includes detailed transcriptions of tunes, exactly as recorded by:

Ray Barretto	Irakere	Andy Narell	Ft. Apache Band	Djavan
Eddie Palmieri	Celia Cruz	Mario Bauza	Dave Valentin	Tom Jobim
Fania All-Stars	Arsenio Rodriguez	Dizzy Gilllespie	Paquito D'Rivera	Toninho Horta
Tito Puente	Tito Rodriguez	Mongo Santamaria	Clare Fischer	Joao Bosco
Ruben Blades	Orquesta Aragon	Manny Oquendo & Libre	Chick Corea	Milton Nascimento
Los Van Van	Beny Moré	Puerto Rico All-Stars	Sergio Mendes	Leila Pinheiro
NG La Banda	Cal Tjader	Issac Delgaldo	Ivan Lins	Gal Costa
				And Many More!

Muy Caliente!

Afro-Cuban Play-Along CD and Book

Rebeca Mauleón - Keyboard
Oscar Stagnaro - Bass
Orestes Vilató - Timbales
Carlos Caro - Bongos
Edgardo Cambon - Congas

(Over 70 min. of smokin' Latin grooves)

The Latin Real Book Sampler CD

12 of the greatest Latin Real Book tunes as played by the original artists: Tito Puente, Ray Barretto, Andy Narell, Puerto Rico Allstars, Bacacoto, etc. $16 list price. Available in U.S.A. only.

101 Montunos

by **Rebeca Mauleón**

The only comprehensive study of Latin piano playing ever published.

- Bi-lingual text (English/Spanish)
- 2 CDs of the author demonstrating each montuno
- Covers over 100 years of Afro-Cuban styles, including the danzón, guaracha, mambo, merengue and songo—from Peruchin to Eddie Palmieri.

The True Cuban Bass

By **Carlos Del Puerto,** (bassist with Irakere) and **Silvio Vergara**, $22.

For acoustic or electric bass; English and Spanish text; Includes CDs of either historic Cuban recordings or Carlos playing each exercise; Many transcriptions of complete bass parts for tunes in different Cuban styles – the roots of Salsa.

The Brazilian Guitar Book

by **Nelson Faria**, one of Brazil's best new guitarists.

- Over 140 pages of comping patterns, transcriptions and chord melodies for samba, bossa, baiaõ, etc.
- Complete chord voicings written out for each example.
- Comes with a CD of Nelson playing each example.
- The most complete Brazilian guitar method ever published! $26 including surface postage.

Joe Diorio – "Nelson Faria's book is a welcome addition to the guitar literature. I'm sure those who work with this volume wiill benefit greatly"

The Salsa Guide Book

By **Rebeca Mauleón**

The only complete method book on salsa ever published! 260 pages. $25

Carlos Santana – "A true treasure of knowledge and information about Afro-Cuban music."
Mark Levine, author of The *Jazz Piano Book*. – "This the book on salsa."
Sonny Bravo, pianist with Tito Puente – "This will be salsa 'bible' for years to come."
Oscar Hernández, pianist with Rubén Blades – "An excellent and much needed resource."

The New Real Book Series

The Standards Real Book (C only)

Alice In Wonderland
All Of You
Alone Together
At Last
Baltimore Oriole
A Beautiful Friendship
Bess, You Is My Woman
But Not For Me
Close Enough For Love
Crazy He Calls Me
Dancing In The Dark
Days Of Wine And Roses
Dreamsville
Easy To Love
Embraceable You

Falling In Love With Love
From This Moment On
Give Me The Simple Life
Have You Met Miss Jones?
Hey There
I Can't Get Started
I Concentrate On You
I Cover The Waterfront
I Love You
I Loves You Porgy
I Only Have Eyes For You
I Wish I Knew
I'm A Fool To Want You
Indian Summer

It Ain't Necessarily So
It Never Entered My Mind
It's You Or No One
Just One Of Those Things
Love For Sale
Love Walked In
Lover, Come Back To Me
The Man I Love
Mr. Lucky
My Funny Valentine
My Heart Stood Still
My Man's Gone Now
Old Folks
On A Clear Day

Our Love Is Here To Stay
Secret Love
September In The Rain
Serenade In Blue
Shiny Stockings
Since I Fell For You
So In Love
So Nice (Summer Samba)
Some Other Time
Stormy Weather
The Summer Knows
Summer Night
Summertime
Teach Me Tonight

That Sunday, That Summer
Then I'll Be Tired Of You
There's No You
A Time For Love
Time On My Hands
'Tis Autumn
Where Or When
Who Cares?
With A Song In My Heart
You Go To My Head
Ain't No Sunshine
'Round Midnight
The Girl From Ipanema
Bluesette
And Hundreds More!

The New Real Book - Volume 1 (C, Bb or Eb)

Angel Eyes
Anthropology
Autumn Leaves
Beautiful Love
Bernie's Tune
Blue Bossa
Blue Daniel
But Beautiful
Chain Of Fools
Chelsea Bridge
Compared To What
Darn That Dream
Desafinado
Early Autumn
Eighty One

E.S.P.
Everything Happens To Me
Fall
Feel Like Makin' Love
Footprints
Four
Four On Six
Gee Baby Ain't I Good To
You
Gone With The Wind
Here's That Rainy Day
I Love Lucy
I Mean You
I Should Care
I Thought About You

If I Were A Bell
Imagination
The Island
Jersey Bounce
Joshua
Lady Bird
Like Someone In Love
Line For Lyons
Little Sunflower
Lush Life
Mercy, Mercy, Mercy
The Midnight Sun
Monk's Mood
Moonlight In Vermont
My Shining Hour

Nature Boy
Nefertiti
Nothing Personal
Oleo
Once I Loved
Out Of This World
Pent Up House
Polkadots And
Moonbeams
Portrait Of Tracy
Put It Where You Want It
Robbin's Nest
Ruby, My Dear
Satin Doll
Search For Peace

Shaker Song
Skylark
A Sleepin' Bee
Solar
Speak No Evil
St. Thomas
Street Life
Tenderly
These Foolish Things
This Masquerade
Three Views Of A Secret
Waltz For Debby
Willow Weep For Me
And Many More!

The New Real Book - Volume 2 (C, Bb or Eb)

Afro-Centric
After You've Gone
Along Came Betty
Bessie's Blues
Black Coffee
Blues For Alice
Body And Soul
Bolivia
The Boy Next Door
Bye Bye Blackbird
Cherokee
A Child Is Born
Cold Duck Time
Day By Day

Django
Equinox
Exactly Like You
Falling Grace
Five Hundred Miles High
Freedom Jazz Dance
Giant Steps
Got A Match?
Harlem Nocturne
Hi-Fly
Honeysuckle Rose
I Hadn't Anyone 'Til You
I'll Be Around
I'll Get By

Ill Wind
I'm Glad There Is You
Impressions
In Your Own Sweet Way
It's The Talk Of The Town
Jordu
Killer Joe
Lullaby Of The Leaves
Manha De Carneval
The Masquerade Is Over
Memories Of You
Moment's Notice
Mood Indigo
My Ship

Naima
Nica's Dream
Once In A While
Perdido
Rosetta
Sea Journey
Senor Blues
September Song
Seven Steps To Heaven
Silver's Serenade
So Many Stars
Some Other Blues
Song For My Father
Sophisticated Lady

Spain
Stablemates
Stardust
Sweet And Lovely
That's All
There Is No Greater Love
'Til There Was You
Time Remembered
Turn Out The Stars
Unforgettable
While We're Young
Whisper Not
Will You Still Be Mine?
You're Everything
And Many More!

The New Real Book - Volume 3 (C, Bb, Eb or Bass clef)

Actual Proof
Ain't That Peculair
Almost Like Being In Love
Another Star
Autumn Serenade
Bird Of Beauty
Black Nile
Blue Moon
Butterfly
Caravan
Ceora
Close Your Eyes
Creepin'
Day Dream

Dolphin Dance
Don't Be That Way
Don't Blame Me
Emily
Everything I Have Is
Yours
For All We Know
Freedomland
The Gentle Rain
Get Ready
A Ghost Of A Chance
Heat Wave
How Sweet It Is
I Fall In Love Too Easily

I Got It Bad
I Hear A Rhapsody
If You Could See Me Now
In A Mellow Tone
In A Sentimental Mood
Inner Urge
Invitation
The Jitterbug Waltz
Just Friends
Just You, Just Me
Knock On Wood
The Lamp Is Low
Laura
Let's Stay Together
Litha

Lonely Woman
Maiden Voyage
Moon And Sand
Moonglow
My Girl
On Green Dolphin Street
Over The Rainbow
Prelude To A Kiss
Respect
Ruby
The Second Time Around
Serenata
The Shadow Of Your Smile
So Near, So Far
Solitude

Speak Like A Child
Spring Is Here
Stairway To The Stars
Star Eyes
Stars Fell On Alabama
Stompin' At The Savoy
Sugar
Sweet Lorraine
Taking A Chance On Love
This Is New
Too High
(Used To Be A) Cha Cha
When Lights Are Low
You Must Believe In Spring
And Many More!

Other Jazz Publications

The Jazz Theory Book

By Mark Levine, the most comprehensive Jazz Theory book ever published! $38 list price.
- Over 500 pages of text and over 750 musical examples.
- Written in the language of the working jazz musician, this book is easy to read and user-friendly. At the same time, it is the most comprehensive study of jazz harmony and theory ever published.
- Mark Levine has worked with Bobby Hutcherson, Cal Tjader, Joe Henderson, Woody Shaw, and many other jazz greats.

The Jazz Piano Book

By Mark Levine, Concord recording artist and pianist with Cal Tjader. For beginning to advanced pianists. The only truly comprehensive method ever published. Over 300 pages. $28

Richie Beirach – "The best new method book available."
Hal Galper – "This is a must!"
Jamey Aebersold – "This is an invaluable resource for any pianist."
James Williams – "One of the most complete anthologies on jazz piano."

The Improvisor's Bass Method

By Chuck Sher. A complete method for electric or acoustic bass, plus transcribed solos and bass lines by Mingus, Jaco, Ron Carter, Scott LaFaro, Paul Jackson, Ray Brown, and more! Over 200 pages. $16

International Society of Bassists – "Undoubtedly the finest book of its kind."

Eddie Gomez – "Informative, readily comprehensible and highly imaginative"

Concepts For Bass Soloing

By Chuck Sher and Marc Johnson, (bassist with Bill Evans, etc.) The only book ever published that is specifically designed to improve your soloing! $26
- Includes two CDs of Marc Johnson soloing on each exercise
- Transcriptions of bass solos by: Eddie Gomez, John Patitucci, Scott LaFaro, Jimmy Haslip, etc.

"It's a pleasure to encounter a Bass Method so well conceived and executed." – **Steve Swallow**

The Yellowjackets Songbook

Complete package contains six separate spiral-bound books, one each for:
- Piano/partial score • C melody lead sheet
- Synthesizer/miscellaneous parts
- Bb & Eb Horn melody part • Bass • Drums

Contains 20 great tunes from their entire career. Charts exactly as recorded – approved by the Yellowjackets. World famous Sher Music Co. accuracy and legibility. Over 400 pages, $38 list price.

The Jazz Solos of Chick Corea

Over 150 pages of Chick's greatest solos; "Spain", "Litha", "Windows", "Sicily", etc. for all instrumentalists, single line transcriptions, not full piano score. $18

Chick Corea – "I don't know anyone I would trust more to correctly transcribe my improvisations."

The World's Greatest Fake Book

Jazz & Fusion Tunes by: **Coltrane, Mingus, Jaco, Chick Corea, Bird, Herbie Hancock, Bill Evans, McCoy, Beirach, Ornette, Wayne Shorter, Zawinul, AND MANY MORE!** $32

Chick Corea – "Great for any students of jazz.'
Dave Liebman – "The fake book of the 80's."
George Cables – "The most carefully conceived fake book I've ever seen."

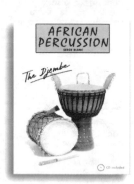

African Percussion, The Djembe

The first comprehensive djembe method book ever published.
- CD included of the author, Serge Blanc, playing each section of the book.
- Includes 22 great standards of traditional djembe music.
- Duet and trios writtten out so you can start playing and practising in groups.

Now Available in CD Format! - The New Real Book Play-Along CDs (For Volume 1)

CD #1 - Jazz Classics - Lady Bird, Bouncin' With Bud, Up Jumped Spring, Monk's Mood, Doors, Very Early, Eighty One, Voyage **& More!**
CD #2 - Choice Standards - Beautiful Love, Darn That Dream, Moonlight In Vermont, Trieste, My Shining Hour, I Should Care **& More!**
CD #3 - Pop-Fusion - Morning Dance, Nothing Personal, La Samba, Hideaway, This Masquerade, Three Views Of A Secret, Rio **& More!**
World-Class Rhythm Sections, featuring Mark Levine, Larry Dunlap, Sky Evergreen, Bob Magnusson, Keith Jones, Vince Lateano & Tom Hayashi

---